US MILITARY

US ARMY

BY ANITA BANKS

WWW.APEXEDITIONS.COM

Copyright © 2023 by Apex Editions, Mendota Heights, MN 55120. All rights reserved. No part of this book may be reproduced or utilized in any form or by any means without written permission from the publisher.

Apex is distributed by North Star Editions:
sales@northstareditions.com | 888-417-0195

Produced for Apex by Red Line Editorial.

Photographs ©: Shutterstock Images, cover, 1, 4–5, 6–7, 8–9, 16–17, 20, 22–23, 24, 24–25, 26, 27, 29; iStockphoto, 10–11, 12, 14–15, 18–19; U.S. Army/Wikimedia Commons, 21

Library of Congress Control Number: 2022901413

ISBN
978-1-63738-311-7 (hardcover)
978-1-63738-347-6 (paperback)
978-1-63738-415-2 (ebook pdf)
978-1-63738-383-4 (hosted ebook)

Printed in the United States of America
Mankato, MN
082022

NOTE TO PARENTS AND EDUCATORS

Apex books are designed to build literacy skills in striving readers. Exciting, high-interest content attracts and holds readers' attention. The text is carefully leveled to allow students to achieve success quickly. Additional features, such as bolded glossary words for difficult terms, help build comprehension.

TABLE OF CONTENTS

CHAPTER 1
SNEAK ATTACK 4

CHAPTER 2
HISTORY OF THE ARMY 10

CHAPTER 3
RANKS AND TRAINING 16

CHAPTER 4
GEAR AND GADGETS 22

COMPREHENSION QUESTIONS • 28
GLOSSARY • 30
TO LEARN MORE • 31
ABOUT THE AUTHOR • 31
INDEX • 32

CHAPTER 1

SNEAK ATTACK

A US Army plane flies high above enemy land. The door opens. Army Rangers **parachute** down through the night sky.

Soldiers who are trained to jump out of planes are called paratroopers.

The only light is from the moon. The Army Rangers land near an enemy hideout. They join other soldiers on the ground.

SPECIAL FORCES

In addition to regular soldiers, the US Army has special forces. These groups include Army Rangers and Green Berets. These soldiers go through extra training. Then, they do difficult missions.

Army Rangers lead other soldiers on special missions.

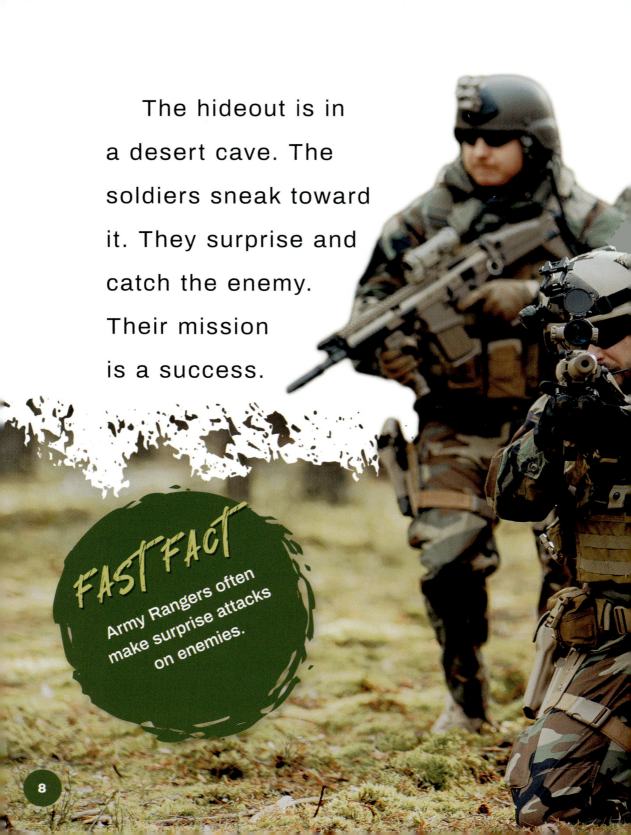

The hideout is in a desert cave. The soldiers sneak toward it. They surprise and catch the enemy. Their mission is a success.

FAST FACT
Army Rangers often make surprise attacks on enemies.

Army soldiers must work together to reach their goals.

CHAPTER 2

History of the Army

The Army was formed in 1775. Early soldiers fought in the Revolutionary War (1775–1783). At the time, America was a British **colony**. The soldiers fought to make it **independent**.

More than 230,000 soldiers served in the US Army during the Revolutionary War.

Since then, the Army has defended the United States. Army soldiers have fought in many wars. They have guarded US land and attacked US enemies.

FAST FACT
The Army's motto is "This We'll Defend." It was first used in 1778.

◀ The US Army fought against Japan, Germany, and Italy during World War II (1939–1945).

Army soldiers also help US **allies**. Soldiers travel to other countries. There, they help fight or keep peace.

WORKING WITH ALLIES

The US Army often works with other countries. It may help them get information. It may send them weapons or supplies. Its troops may also help fight a shared enemy.

The US Army often helps in South Korea. This country is one ally of the United States.

CHAPTER 3

RANKS AND TRAINING

The Army has more than 20 **ranks** of soldiers and officers. Private is the lowest rank. To become privates, people must go through boot camp.

Soldiers learn how to shoot, fight, and survive during boot camp.

After boot camp, Army soldiers can do many jobs. Some drive vehicles. Some build or fix equipment. Others give medical care.

FAST FACT

The Army is the largest US military branch. It had about 485,000 active soldiers in 2021.

Being a pilot is one job option for people who join the Army.

Some soldiers train to become officers. They learn to lead other soldiers. Officers can earn higher ranks. The top rank is general.

Officers can plan missions and tell soldiers what to do.

Military dogs must go through a lot of training to work in the Army.

MILITARY DOGS

Dogs do many jobs in the Army. Some dogs attack enemies. Others help with search and rescue missions. Soldiers train and care for them.

CHAPTER 4

GEAR AND GADGETS

Army soldiers do many kinds of missions. So, they use many types of gear. Each soldier carries gear in a **rucksack**.

A soldier's rucksack can weigh up to 80 pounds (36 kg) when full.

Soldiers often carry Meals Ready to Eat (MREs) for food.

Soldiers pack different gear depending on the type of mission. They always pack weapons and radios. Sometimes they pack night-vision goggles. These goggles help soldiers see in the dark.

Army soldiers wear helmets and eye gear for protection.

FAST FACT

Some Army soldiers fly drones. These aircraft don't have pilots. People control them from the ground.

Army soldiers also use many types of vehicles. Some fly in helicopters or airplanes. Others drive trucks or tanks. These vehicles carry weapons, soldiers, and supplies.

Tanks are often used in battle. The thick metal sides protect soldiers inside.

A Black Hawk helicopter can fly 183 miles per hour (295 km/h).

BLACK HAWKS

Army soldiers often use UH-60 Black Hawks. These helicopters can carry heavy loads. They can also use many weapons. They can shoot guns and missiles.

COMPREHENSION QUESTIONS

Write your answers on a separate piece of paper.

1. Write a sentence describing one mission an Army soldier might do.

2. There are many jobs within the US Army. Which job would you most like to have? Why?

3. When was the Army formed?
    - **A.** 1775
    - **B.** 1778
    - **C.** 2021

4. Why would the Army need many types of vehicles?
    - **A.** Its soldiers can't carry gear.
    - **B.** Its soldiers don't travel very far.
    - **C.** Its missions take place in many different places.

5. What does **defended** mean in this book?

Since then, the Army has defended the United States. Army soldiers have fought in many wars.

    A. fought to keep something safe
    B. ran away from something
    C. tried to get rid of something

6. What does **vehicles** mean in this book?

Army soldiers also use many types of vehicles. Some fly in helicopters or airplanes.

    A. types of plants
    B. machines that carry people and things
    C. machines that make food

Answer key on page 32.

GLOSSARY

allies
Groups or countries that agree to work together or help one another.

colony
An area ruled by a different country.

independent
Not ruled or controlled by another country.

missiles
Flying weapons that explode.

missions
Important tasks or goals.

parachute
To jump from high up while wearing fabric to slow one's fall.

ranks
Levels of power or importance.

rucksack
A large backpack that soldiers use to carry supplies.

BOOKS

Bassier, Emma. *Military Gear.* Minneapolis: Abdo Publishing, 2020.

Pagel-Hogan, Elizabeth. *US Special Operations Forces Equipment and Vehicles*. Minneapolis: Abdo Publishing, 2021.

Vonder Brink, Tracy. *The United States Army*. North Mankato, MN: Capstone Publishing, 2021.

ONLINE RESOURCES

Visit **www.apexeditions.com** to find links and resources related to this title.

ABOUT THE AUTHOR

Anita Banks lives and writes in North Alabama. She loves reading, hiking, and running. She also loves to travel and learn new things.

INDEX

A
allies, 14–15
Army Rangers, 4, 6, 8

B
boot camp, 16, 18

D
dogs, 21
drones, 25

E
enemies, 4, 6, 8, 13, 15, 21

G
Green Berets, 6

M
mission, 6, 8, 21, 22, 24
motto, 13

O
officers, 16, 20

P
private, 16

R
Revolutionary War, 10
rucksack, 22

V
vehicles, 18, 26–27

W
weapons, 15, 24, 27

ANSWER KEY:
1. Answers will vary; 2. Answers will vary; 3. A; 4. C; 5. A; 6. B